T.S. CHERRY

You are that Tree

The Garden of Eden (Answers Book 1)

First published by Tiil Books 2019

Copyright © 2019 by T.S. Cherry

All rights reserved. No part of this publication may be reproduced, stored or transmitted in any form or by any means, electronic, mechanical, photocopying, recording, scanning, or otherwise without written permission from the publisher. It is illegal to copy this book, post it to a website, or distribute it by any other means without permission.

T.S. Cherry asserts the moral right to be identified as the author of this work.

First edition

This book was professionally typeset on Reedsy.
Find out more at reedsy.com

*This is dedicated to my Children. May your understanding be enlightened and truth
light your path to success.*

Contents

INTRODUCTION   iii

I   You are That Tree

YOU ARE THAT TREE	3
FOR GOD'S GLORY	5
MOVE AWAY	9
PUT GOD IN CHARGE	13
GOOD DECISIONS OR GODLY DECISIONS	16

II   The Apple

A STRUGGLE EXISTS	21
THE APPLE	27

III   Don't Bite The Apple

WHAT SHOULD I EXPECT?	37
DIVINE TIMING	43
SOUND OF THE TRUMPET	48

IV Angels and Snakes

SNAKES AND ANGELS   63
IDENTIFYING VOICES   73
IT'S ALL ABOUT HIS WILL   80

V Book 2

INTRODUCTION

INTRODUCTION

In the middle of the garden were **the tree of life** *and* **the tree of the knowledge of good and evil.** *Genesis 2:9, NIV*

You are the Tree! is an exposé on the two trees in the Garden of Eden. It is a non-traditional or unconventional exposition of God's infallible Word on *The Tree of Life* and *The Tree of the Knowledge of Good and Evil*. It is divided into four main parts containing twelve life-changing chapters.

The first part, **You are the Tree**, opens up on the significance of the tree in the middle of the Garden. What is the meaning behind the *Tree of Life*? What is the purpose of the *tree of the knowledge of good and evil*? What do they mean to our lives?

You will get to know that you have the power within you either to be the *tree of life* - which is the expression of God through flesh - or the *tree of good and evil*. While one connects you to God, the other separates you from God, His wisdom, and ultimately, His purpose for your life.

The second part, **The Apple**, deals with *the forbidden apple*, which is the "way without God; the path of self; the way of disobedience." This was "the apple" that Eve and Sarah presented before their husbands and the men bought into it, without considering the deadly consequences that went with giving that "apple" a bite.

This book will help you to look deeply inward and try to find the "apples" in your life. It will help you to carefully re-evaluate every decision you've ever made. Was God in it or was it just you?

The third part, **Don't Bite the Apple**, addresses the consequences of *"giving the forbidden apple a bite,"* which is to make a decision to follow our own path in life, instead of God's. Eve gave the apple a bite while Mary didn't. From the products of their conception, we learn that what we create or birth on earth, is a result of whether we *bite the apple* or not. The last part of the book, **Snakes and Angels**, is a profound exposition on how to put the "snakes" – the wrong voices and influences - out of our garden. It presents *how to differentiate between the voice of the snake and that of God*, which is the first major struggle of many people.

It is my prayer, that this book will greatly deepen your knowledge of God and help you to exercise the authority of bringing the things 'you are pregnant with' from the spirit realm to the natural realm. I pray that you will find help to fulfill Divine purpose and bring glory to God.

Shalom!

T.S CHERRY

I

You are That Tree

The first part, **You are the Tree**, *opens up on the significance of the tree in the middle of the Garden. What is the meaning behind the Tree of Life? What is the purpose of the tree of the knowledge of good and evil? What do they mean to our lives?*

1

YOU ARE THAT TREE

The tree you saw was growing very tall and strong, reaching high into the heavens for all the world to see. It had fresh green leaves and was loaded with fruit for all to eat. Wild animals lived in its shade, and birds nested in its branches. **That tree, Your Majesty, is you.**
Daniel 4:20-22, NLT

Daniel the Beloved, in unraveling the king's dream about a tree, reveals that "the king is the tree." And that is God's Word to you too: "You are the Tree."

I tried to find an example to help each person understand the use of the term "majesty" in our anchor Scripture above, because often times, in the Body of Faith the idea of the 'king' and the 'kingdom' have a different meaning than it does from the usage in this text.

If you think about it, the position of the President of the United States is also a military position because it has similar functions to that of a military position. The similarity lies in the fact that in both instances, when you retire from the position, you maintain whatever your highest rank is. In the case of the President, his highest rank would be 'The President.'

Also, in the military, if you retire with 'captain' as your highest rank, that is the position with which you will be addressed. In other words, my husband who retired as a captain, is still addressed as 'Captain Cherry,' even though he no longer holds the position and no longer has the power and authority of a serving captain.

Now, the Bible addresses us as 'Kings and Priests.' So, many believers still retain their title as 'Majesty' even when they have moved out of the position of power and authority. In other words, they have a job, but they haven't assumed the position of authority as yet. They have business to do, but they don't know how to take it to the next level. Yes, they aren't slaves, but they aren't in a position of power either. It is clear they have made some progress, but they are clearly digressing too.

So, it's more like, "I look better on the outside, but Satan is attacking my emotions and is basically running my life." Or, "I have declared the kingship and blessings, but it hasn't manifested in my life."

If that describes you, the message of this book is for you. I want you to know that you are the tree in the midst of the garden. This message has changed my perspective of things and I'm hoping that it will bless you as well and bring real change to your life, destiny, and ultimately, your relationship with God.

2

FOR GOD'S GLORY

I was doing some studying on Daniel the prophet and I realized that Daniel's interpretation to Nebuchadnezzar's dream seemed familiar. Upon examination I realized why, it seemed to be closely related to the Tree in the Garden of Eden. In studying a bit deeper, I reread the Book of Genesis and realized it actually begins much like a dream.

It occurred to me that perhaps Nebuchadnezzar was asking for the meaning of what occurred back in Genesis. What is the meaning behind the tree of life? What is the purpose of the other tree in the midst of the Garden - the tree of knowledge of good and evil? What does this mean to our lives?

Notice how God created each of the trees in the midst of the Garden for a specific purpose. Most scholars believe that if man had eaten of the tree of life, he would probably live forever. The tree of life was meant to supply the fullness of life.

The tree of knowledge of good and evil was also there to test man's resolve to obey God. Remember that God had created man as a free moral agent. Man had free will. The common belief is that the tree of knowledge of good and evil was a good test of how much man was willing to make the choice to obey God at will. It was a test of man's positive choice or decision in the direction of pleasing his Maker.

When you look at the fact that God made the trees in the Garden with a specific purpose in mind, you will better understand the tree in Daniel's vision as being stationed specifically for the manifestation of God's glory.

The Bible says, "*I saw a large tree in the middle of the earth. The tree grew very tall and strong, reaching high into the heavens for all the world to see. It had fresh green leaves, and **it was loaded with fruit for all to eat**. Wild animals lived in its shade, and birds nested in its branches. **All the world was fed from this tree.**"* **Daniel 4:10-12, NLT**

The nature of this tree opens up a whole new understanding or thinking that can be applied to your business life and to your personal life. Take note of a few things about this tree:

> *It was a large tree in the middle of the earth;*
> *It grew tall and strong, reaching high into the heavens for all the world to see.*
> *It had fresh green leaves loaded with fruits for all to eat.*
> *Wild animals lived in its shade and birds nested in its branches*
> *All the world was fed from this tree.*

I want you to know that you are the tree in the midst of the garden. Every description of this tree was meant to fit the ideal life God has designed for you to live. You were made to fulfill a specific purpose that brings glory to God. You were meant to walk in the promises of God and let your testimony challenge many to serve the Lord. But most of the times, this is not the case.

The Bible describes this tree as "a large tree in the middle of the earth." Beloved, you are meant to be 'a large tree' in the midst of your family, your business, ministry, work place, and in fact everything you do. You are meant to occupy the central position, the peak. You are meant, as Moses said, to be ABOVE ONLY!

Notice that the Bible says the tree, "grew tall and strong, reaching high into the heavens *for all the world to see.*" See that? "For all the world to see!" That's the description of your life, the real way God wants your life to be. He wants you to be in such a blessed position that 'all the world' – everyone around you and beyond - can see what He's doing in and with your life.

The Bible tells us that this tree had 'fresh leaves and was loaded with fruits.' It was not like the tree in the New Testament that had fresh leaves all over it which bear no fruits. Mark 11:13-14 says, "*He noticed a fig tree in full leaf a little way off, so he went over to see if he could find any figs.* **But there were only leaves**... *Then Jesus said to the tree, "May no one ever eat your fruit again!*" That tree ended up being cursed.

That's not the picture of life God has for us. He wants us to live in a way that brings blessings to others. He doesn't want us to just look like we have it. He wants us to actually have it and walk in it. He doesn't want us to merely carry a title. He wants us to move up to that realm where we're experiencing the manifestation of His promises in our lives.

God wants us to be in that realm where we are providing shade to both friends and foes. He wants us to be in that place where the whole world is feeding from 'our tree.' So, when you look at that tree in the midst of the field, you see a picture of yourself. You see a picture of where God wants you to be. You see a picture of your next level.

God is challenging you to take your life, your business, your academic pursuit, your finances, etc., to the next level. You were not made for the low places of the earth. You were made for the top most height. But how do you get to experience that next level? In the next chapter, I will show you how!

3

MOVE AWAY

In trying to move our lives to the next level, we have to begin to move away. Yes, I mean it! Move away.

I'd love to explain this with the familiar story of the blind man in Bethsaida. Mark 8:22-26 says, "When they arrived at Bethsaida, some people brought a blind man to Jesus, and they begged him to touch the man and heal him. **Jesus took the blind man by the hand and led him out of the village.** Then, spitting on the man's eyes, he laid his hands on him and asked, "Can you see anything now?" **The man looked around. "Yes," he said, "I see people, but I can't see them very clearly. They look like trees walking around."** Then Jesus placed his hands on the man's eyes again, and his eyes were opened. His sight was completely restored, and he could see everything clearly. Jesus sent him away, saying, "Don't go back into the village on your way home."

There's something about this blind man's miracle. After Jesus prayed for him, he began to see people around him but not clearly. Like this man, up until now, you will notice you haven't been seeing yourself and the people around you clearly. Personally, I began to realize that I didn't have a clear vision of the people that I was surrounding myself with.

Prior to this, notice what Jesus did: He took the blind man, and basically led Him out of the village. The village here is as simple as his tribe. So, Jesus got him away from the people that he considered to be his tribe, so that He could actually help him see things differently.

You know, sometimes when we are with the people of our tribe, we begin to see things from a tribal perspective. But Jesus wanted this man to take a step forward. He didn't want him to see things from a tribal perspective. He wanted him to begin to see from the perspective of God.

So you see what I said at the beginning – move away. Stop seeing from your perspective and that of those around you. If you want to move to the next level, step forward. Move away from the familiar to the Godly. Move away from what you always know how to do, to what God wants you to do. Stop depending on the people around you and learn dependence on God.

BE HUMBLE

Next thing Jesus does after leading this man away from the village is that He spits on his eyes and asks him if he could see anything. This is very humbling. To spit on a person's eyes is basically to lower what that person thinks of himself. It means to reduce everything you thought you knew. Perhaps, Paul explains it better than me when he said,

> ***Philippians 3:8*** What is more, I consider everything a loss because of the surpassing worth of knowing Christ Jesus my Lord, for whose sake I have lost all things. **I consider them**

garbage, that I may gain Christ.

So, when Jesus spit in his eye he reduced all his knowledge to garbage.

The willingness to accept Jesus spitting in your eye, how you see things, your perspective requires real humility. But beloved, if you really want to change your life, you must be ready to humble yourself to the place where you will accept the truth, even when it feels like it's being 'spit in to your eye.' Without this, it'll be difficult to have God lead you to the next level where all things can be much clearer to you.

MEN LIKE TREES
Now notice that, as Jesus lays His hands on this man, the first thing he sees are men walking around like trees. First, you have to be able to realize that initially that is the position meant for us. We are meant to be the trees in the midst of the garden.

We are meant to be oozing life and blessings to the people around us. What happens is that most of these men are merely walking around as trees but have lost their authority. They are not exercising their mandate as Daniel described in the last chapter. They are no longer commanders of the blessing. They can't provide food or shade for the wild animals. They merely bear the name.

So, God is challenging you to be that tree in the midst of the garden that Daniel is talking about. You are the tree of life because you carry the life of the Savior in you. John helps us to clearly identify that Jesus in our lives makes us bring life to everyone we come in contact with. The Bible says, "*In him was life; and the life was the light of men*" (John 1:4). What we have received spiritually, we are meant to establish in the natural.

John 5:19 says, "*Then answered Jesus and said unto them, Verily, verily, I say unto you, The Son can do nothing of himself, but what he seeth the Father do: for what things soever he doeth, these also doeth the Son likewise."* In essence, Jesus was doing in the physical what He saw the Father do in the spiritual. He was mirroring what was already done. God had already ordained it in the spirit and what Jesus was doing was taking it from the spirit and manifesting it in the material world.

So, you want to move to the next level? You want the new position at the company? You want to go from working for someone else to working for yourself? You need to understand that you are that tree, and you must exercise the authority of bringing things from the spirit realm to the natural realm, whatever it takes.

Learning from the encounter of the blind man, there's a needed separation from the people around you for some time. There's a needed separation in order to see things from the Divine perspective and speak them forth into existence.

Such separation may include days of fasting or deeper studies in the Word of God in order to hear clearly what God has in mind for your life. However, as long as you need to experience the next level in your life, you must move away from your people for a time, like Jesus did with that blind man. Never forget this principle, and never take it for granted.

4

PUT GOD IN CHARGE

This is basically where you change positions. You want to access the pre-ordained plan of God for your life. You want to know what He created in the spirit so that you begin to fully manifest it in the natural. You don't want to be that tree full of leaves but without fruit, that is finally cursed.

Think about that for a minute. In King Nebuchadnezzar's dream he says, "*I saw in the visions of my head upon my bed, and, behold, a watcher and an holy one came down from heaven; He cried aloud, and said thus,* **Hew down the tree, and cut off his branches***, shake off his leaves, and scatter his fruit: let the beasts get away from under it, and the fowls from his branches:*" Daniel 4:13, 14

Nebuchadnezzar lost his place because he was out of step with God's grace by means of his decisions and utterances.

You see, a person can be a tree but his decisions can cost him his position. Think about it, Adam and Eve were planted in the Garden of God. But they stopped seeking God and started listening to the serpent. Then they began to operate under a curse.

That was how Nebuchadnezzar lost his position and came under a curse. And the curse was that he would graze with the beast of the field until seven years had passed.

Daniel said, *"This is the interpretation, O king, and this is the decree of the most High, which is come upon my lord the king: That they shall drive thee from men, and thy dwelling shall be with the beasts of the field, and they shall make thee to eat grass as oxen, and they shall wet thee with the dew of heaven, and seven times shall pass over thee,* **till thou know that the most High ruleth in the kingdom of men, and giveth it to whomsoever he will"** **Daniel 4:24-25**

Nebuchadnezzar gave the place or glory that was due to God to himself and the result was drastic. God doesn't want you to make the same mistakes. You see, God wants to be the greatest influence over your life. But most of the time, you allow people to influence you that shouldn't. You give people positions in your life that they have no business being in. You delegate power to others over your life. You give people authority over your life instead of having power over your own life. This is what God wants you to sort out.

God wants to be the center of your life. He wants to have first place. He wants to be in charge. He wants to be your first priority. God does not want you to make your decisions and then come ask Him to bless them. He wants it the other way around. God wants to make the decisions and you are blessed when you choose between the tree of life and the tree of knowledge of good and evil, which are both within you.

Remember that when you walk out of God's Word and make wrong choices, you feed the choices to everyone you are connected to. And the result is you miss the mark of where you are supposed to be.

Of course, the devil – that old serpent – will tell you that you won't die if you make the wrong decision. So you make the decision and it takes you further and further away from the Garden to the place where you lose all of your authority.

All of that can change when you choose to put God in charge and see things from His perspective. Learn to prioritize His Word. Let your decisions be based on what He says, not just what you think is right. That is the best recipe for acceleration to your next level.

5

GOOD DECISIONS OR GODLY DECISIONS

How do we move from one place, one position to the next? How do we begin to change our life? It's simple: We stop making good decisions and begin to make Godly decisions.

Now, some of the people you think are trees are not trees at all. Some of them have been cut down. They only have a title as 'believer,' without the accompanying authority. They no longer put God's choices over their own.

This played out in the lives of the Jews when they were asked to choose between the Prince of life and a notorious criminal. Matthew 27:17,20-21 says, "*Therefore when they were gathered together, Pilate said unto them, Whom will ye that I release unto you? Barabbas, or Jesus which is called Christ? But the chief priests and elders persuaded the multitude that they should ask Barabbas, and destroy Jesus. The governor answered and said unto them, Whether of the twain will ye that I release unto you?* **They said, Barabbas**.*"*

Barabbas is the anti-Christ choice. It's the choice that is not anointed, not pre-ordained. It's the choice where you want to become like God, and you think you know good from evil and can make your own decisions.

Daniel lets us know that such trees have been cut down. They may still have 'Majesty' as a title, but they're no longer living in that position.

Beloved, every time you are in between making a decision whether to glorify God with your life or not, just remember that you are trying to choose between Barabbas and the King of kings.

Do you know how many times you have asked for Barabbas in your life? Do you know how many people in your life are Barabbas? What about your business contacts; how many of them are Barabbas?

You need to begin to change your decisions in the direction of bringing honor to your King, the One Who died that you may live. One of the areas you need to make adequate changes to honor God and move your life forward, is in the people you have around you. You need the right kind of people – suitable people around you.

Geneses 2:20 says, "*So the man gave names to all the livestock the birds in the sky, and all the wild beast animals. But for Adam, **no suitable helper** was found.*" Notice it didn't say there wasn't a helper found; it said it wasn't a 'suitable helper.'

The point I want you to get here is that the reason why you keep taking one step forward and two steps backward is because you're not aligning yourself with suitable people - that's the difference. You have to begin to align yourself with suitable people in your life.

As a tree that is meant to exude all the excellent blessings of God, I implore you to make changes that will bring the needed progress in your life. Make decisions that will help you fulfill your role as the tree in the center of the garden.

Remember that 'you are that tree' and that means you must provide food for all, your family inclusive. You must provide shelter to the wild animals, which are those who don't know any better. It's not the other way round. You don't have to let the serpent suggest your meal and eventually get you put out of the garden.
   No!

You must take your place of authority, and that authority is in being able to do and recognize a Godly decision. You don't have to agree, you just have to recognize that God is Who He said He is, and that His decision takes precedence over yours. You don't know what's best for your life. He does; He sees the results.

So, don't just think that you're going to make any decision you want and do things a certain way. I'm gonna challenge you to sit down and pray about your business plan; to sit down and pray about the book that you wanna write; to sit down and pray about the direction of your company.

That way you will come forth as the tree in the midst of the Garden both in name and in authority. And you will never have to exist as a shadow of yourself!
   Shalom!

II

The Apple

*The second part, **The Apple**, deals with the forbidden apple, which is the "way without God; the path of self; the way of disobedience." This was "the apple" that Eve and Sarah presented before their husbands and the men bought into it, without considering the deadly consequences that went with giving that "apple" a bite.*

6

A STRUGGLE EXISTS

The babies jostled each other within her, and she said, "Why is this happening to me?" Genesis 25:22, NIV

We have established through Daniel, that 'you' are the tree in the midst of the garden. In other words, you have the power within you to be that *tree of life*, which is the expression of God through flesh or to be the tree of good and evil.

According to Jewish mythology, in the Garden of Eden is a tree of life, also called the "Tree of souls" that blossoms and produces new souls. The belief that you are "a soul", a personality that gives thought or timeless consciousness, is something worth pondering.

Solomon gives a simple explanation to it. He says, *"What is happening now has happened before, and what will happen in the future has happened before,"* (Ecclesiastes 3:15, NLT). So then, everything that will happen has already happened, because the soul is our connection to every other soul and is timeless.

This invariably connotes the idea of a connection to God. Genesis 2:7 says, "*And the LORD God formed man of the dust of the ground, and breathed into his nostrils the breath of life; and man became a living soul.*" From this Scripture, God formed a body from the dust of the ground, then He took something out of Himself and put in this clay he had formed, and it became a living being.

In essence, man existed in God first, before he became existent on earth. We began to exist on earth when God formed and gave us a body. Before He gave us a body, He perfectly knew us. That is why He said to Jeremiah, "*Before I formed thee in the belly I knew thee;*" (Jeremiah 1:5a). The implication is that we existed in Him before our lives here on Earth.

So, you were a soul previously without a body, but you were connected to other souls and God gave you a body. From the time you became limited to a body, you went from knowing the things of God to adjusting your knowledge to the needs of the body you were given.

Your body then convinces your soul that you are only as old as your body and the knowledge and connections that you previously have. If your body thinks you are 12, you begin to tilt to the idea that you are 12 years old, when the reality is that you are much older than that.

THE STRUGGLE IS REAL

The Scripture explains this duality in many wonderful ways. But perhaps, none is more relevant than the Biblical story of Jacob, who is also Israel. We see Jacob struggle with being the Tree of Life to his people or being a deceiver - a double-minded fellow, that is, the tree of good and evil. This all begins with Jacob's relationship with his brother Esau, and the struggle to express the blessings of God.

Speaking about Rebecca their mother, the Bible says, *"The babies jostled each other within her, and she said, "Why is this happening to me?"* (Genesis 25:22, NIV) Rebecca goes to enquire from God about the movements in her womb, *"And the Lord told her, "The sons in your womb will become two nations. From the very beginning, the two nations will be rivals. One nation will be stronger than the other; and your older son will serve your younger son.""* (Genesis 25:23, NLT).

If you will pause for a while and think about this, a lot of things will become clearer. God tells Rebekah that she will give birth to twin boys and the older will be servant to the younger. I'm sure you already know like I do, that it's supposed to be the other way round. But you see this reality, not just in the case of Esau and Jacob, but in our lives too.

From all we have seen so far, the soul is pre-existent, and has long existed before the body. The body only comes into the picture at birth, but the soul has always been. So, the soul is the older of the two. No matter how old your body is, it's still not the oldest; the soul is. But we see the reality of what God said about Esau and Jacob playing out between the soul and body.

We find that the body lords over the soul a lot of times. In fact, the Apostle Peter admonishes that we *"abstain from fleshly lusts, which war against the soul;"* (1Peter 2:11). The struggle or fight between the younger and the older, which went on in the womb of Rebecca seems to continue today between the body and the soul.

Let me make a quick analogy: Have you ever gone on a diet? The idea that you went on a diet implies some level of discipline. You were focused. You got everything you needed, and you got rid of all the sugar. In other words, you were like the proper Jewish wife who swept all the yeast out of her house so that there was no leaven left in there. In the same way, you took every temptation out of your house, and didn't have to see anything that could make you rescind on your decision.

Then something happens!

About day three - which is typical - you start craving foods that aren't in front of you. You see, it's not like you were tempted by something you saw, but rather because there is something in your memory. You start craving your favorite foods. Sometimes, it almost seems like you can taste it. That's how vivid your imagination is when you get 'cravings.' For some people, it is seriously over-whelming.

So, do you give into these cravings?

The Bible calls these cravings *leaks and onions*. But there are other areas in your life where there are *leaks and onions*. The question is, what things are you addicted to? They help you understand that the struggle is real!

ONE KING

When we look at the story of Rebecca in the right perspective, we see that there are twins within us jostling for superiority. The soul wants to rule over the body and the body wants to rule over the soul. But the coming of Christ to die for our sins was designed to change all that. The death of Christ was meant to bring both body and soul under the rule of ONE KING, which is Jesus Christ or God's Word.

Ezekiel gives us a clear prophecy of the mind of God on this: He says in Ezekiel 37:22, *"And I will make them one nation in the land upon the mountains of Israel; and one king shall be king to them all: and they shall be no more two nations, neither shall they be divided into two kingdoms any more at all."*

God's mind here is to bring the conflict of the soul and the body under the Lordship of Jesus Christ. Both propensities have to be brought under total submission to the Word of God. When James said, *"Wherefore lay apart all filthiness and superfluity of naughtiness, and receive with meekness the engrafted word, which is able to save your souls"* (James 1:21), he meant that, in principle, only the Word of God can have absolute impact on the soul.

The Apostle Paul writing to the Hebrews about the supremacy of God's Word over both body and soul says, *"For the word of God is alive and powerful. It is sharper than the sharpest two-edged sword, cutting between soul and spirit, between joint and marrow. It exposes our innermost thoughts and desires"* (Hebrews 4:12, NLT).

While "soul and spirit" refer to the pre-existent part of us, "joint and marrow" refer to the body. Paul says that the Word of God bears rule over them all. So, Ezekiel's prophecy comes true: *"and one king shall be king to them all."* We see that the ultimate goal is for us to not be divided, but to be one kingdom, having one king to whom we submit. The idea is that our lives express more of the fruits of the tree of life than of the tree of good and evil.

Now we see that the Holy Spirit dwelling within us is the *Tree of Life* while our flesh is the *Tree of the knowledge of good and evil*. The purpose of the Holy Spirit of God is Truth, the enlightenment of men, etc. The Holy Spirit within us is our connection to God. The Holy Spirit acts as a comforter, One who intercedes, supports or acts as an advocate, particularly in times where we are in trouble, or we are going through trials.

In contrast, the *tree of the knowledge of good and evil* leads to separation. The Book of Proverbs says it better: *"There is a way which seemeth right unto a man, but the end thereof are the ways of death"* (Proverbs 14:12). So, the end result of the tree of good and evil is death – separation. Separation from what? Separation from God, from purpose, from wisdom, and from the knowledge of God.

You see, often times we try to make things happen instead of waiting on God. We become impatient and play God, which doesn't really make things better. In fact, our manipulation of the situation is part of the problem we create. And it never gets better but worse.

Let's take a look at this more practically considering the actions of Eve, Sarah, Rebecca and Jacob in relation to eating the "apple" that was forbidden.

7

THE APPLE

*A**nd when the woman saw that the tree was good for food, and that it was pleasant to the eyes, and a tree to be desired to make one wise, she took of the fruit thereof, and did eat, and gave also unto her husband with her; and he did eat.* Genesis 3:6

First and foremost, I want you to understand that "The forbidden apple" presented here is the "way without God;" the path of self; the way of disobedience. This was the "apple" Eve and Sarah presented before their husbands and they bought into it, without considering the consequences that went with giving that "apple" a bite.

It was the same apple that Rebecca and Jacob partook of, without thinking of the long-term effects of their decisions.

EVE AND SARAH

As the Bible describes it, Sarah is the mother of all nations. That description is very similar to that of Eve, who is the mother of all living.

Besides this, there is a common trend we see between both of them: We see that they both convinced their husbands to bite the "apple." They both displayed doubts concerning God's Word.

Both women had two children, one that was of the promise and one that was sent away. Eve had Cain and Abel. Sarah had Ishmael and Isaac. Both Cain and Ishmael were sent away. Cain went with his wife and Ishmael with his mother.

Cain killed Abel and God sent him out into the open world as a vagabond. Also, once Sarah realized that it's her own son that was supposed to be blessed, took it upon herself to get rid of Ishmael. She made the suggestion to Abraham and both Ishmael and his mother were sent into the wild world to face life. That way, Isaac was able to get the firstborn's blessing from his father.

Of Eve the Bible says in Genesis 3:6 says, *"And when the woman saw that the tree was good for food, and that it was pleasant to the eyes, and a tree to be desired to make one wise, she took of the fruit thereof, and did eat, and gave also unto her husband with her; and he did eat."*

Of Sarah the Bible says in Genesis 16:2, *"And Sarai said unto Abram, Behold now, the LORD hath restrained me from bearing: I pray thee, go in unto my maid; it may be that I may obtain children by her. And Abram hearkened to the voice of Sarai."*

Now, placed side-by-side, it is clear that both women convinced their husbands to bite the apple [a way without God].

Eve first began to doubt the Word of God as she listened to the serpent. Genesis 3:4-5 says, *"And the serpent said unto the woman, Ye shall not surely die: For God doth know that in the day ye eat thereof, then your eyes shall be opened, and ye shall be as gods, knowing good and evil."* As she listened to this, she began to feed the doubt in her heart, and it of course led to her actions of biting the apple. We know this because of the actions she took immediately after she heard from the serpent.

In the same vein, Sarah looks at her state and begins to feed her doubts, despite the Word of God given to Abraham concerning their childless state. She felt that at her age, she wasn't going to be able to have a child. There was doubt in her mind as to whether God was actually going to give her the promised child.

She decided to take a bite on the "apple," too.

Now, we can see the chaotic result of Sarah's "apple:" two children - one she adopted by her handmaid, that is *the tree of good and evil*; and one that came from within her, which was the one she was really meant to have, which is *the Tree of Life*.

My question to you is, has God ever made you a promise and you tried to make it happen by your power? Have you ever gotten tired of waiting on God and decided that you were going to make something happen?

Of course, the reality of is, we all have. We are all guilty of doubting that God was going to do something He took too long to do. So we tried to make it happen or help God out, if you will.

But think about it beloved, God didn't say that the promise would be born from something outside of you. He told you that the promise would come from within the center of you, *the tree of life*. That makes a world of difference.

COULD REBECCA HELP GOD?

As we have already seen, God had promised Rebecca that she would have two children, but the older shall serve the younger. Of course, God alone understood how He was going to bring that to pass. Rather than let God have His way in fulfilling His promise, Rebecca took it upon herself to fulfill God's Word.

Rebecca and Jacob cheated Esau out of his birthright. They took advantage of the blindness of Isaac and made Jacob impersonate Esau, to the end that Esau would be denied of his birthright. That led to a feud that sent Jacob fleeing the country of his birth.

Many years later, Jacob was set to return to his father's house. But he was fully aware that his angry brother was still waiting for him. He decided to seek the face of God. That night, he wrestled with God and forced God to bless him.

Something is worthy of note here. Sometimes we think that because we force God's Hand on something, it is of God. Not necessarily! In other words, if you forced God to give you a child, for instance, it doesn't necessarily mean that the child is God's promise.

The biting of the apple in Rebecca's case is that even though she knew better, that God would come through with His promise, she went ahead and tricked her husband. Her flesh had deceived her into going about things her own way and getting her husband to bless the wrong child. She never knew that by helping Jacob steal his brother's birthright, she was also getting Jacob separated from what was rightfully his.

Just like Sarah, who wanted her son to have the blessings of the first child, Rebecca wanted the same thing for her loving child, Jacob. And she wanted it so much that she tricked Isaac into giving Jacob everything (the blessing), which rightfully belonged to his brother.

JACOB PLAIN MISSED IT

We can clearly see what "the apple" is: Rebecca's willingness to lie, cheat, and steal, all to make sure that her son was in charge. When most people think about Jacob, they think about him as being the blessed one, but the reality is that Jacob bit the apple in order to be in power, and he would later experience the consequences of his actions way down to his grave.

> Some time later Joseph was told, "Your father is ill." So he set out with his two sons, Manasseh and Ephraim. When **Jacob** was told, "Your son Joseph has come to you," **Israel** rallied his strength and sat up in bed. **Jacob** said to Joseph, "God Almighty appeared to me at Luz in the land of Canaan, and there he blessed me. (Genesis 48: 1-3 , NIV)

In other words, **Jacob** who is also **Israel** is not the *tree of life* that he should be to his people. Jacob is the tree of good and evil. That's what he produces in the earth: some good things and some evil things, because he allowed his fleshly desires to dominate him.

What God really wanted for him was to be the tree of life; that is what God CALLED him to be. But he replaced one purpose for another, because he just didn't trust God. He didn't trust that God could fulfill His promised blessing in his life. He doubted God's Word so much that he had to take someone else's blessing.

A PEEP INTO OUR LIVES

In this day and time where people want to be in charge, and people want to determine who gets blessed or who gets what, we don't think about how wrong it is to put people in positions they are not supposed to be in. We take someone else's blessings, put them out of their position, try to devise our own plan, come up with a devious solution, and a wrong seed is sown.

Eventually, what we planted grows up into the tree of both good and evil. We find some seeming good in it, but we also readily see the evil in it.

We must begin to look deeply inward and try to find the "apples" in our lives – that is, where we try to manipulate situations and circumstances to our advantage.

Jacob and his ancestors, Abraham and Sarah, gave birth to something that was not part of them. Yet, they had to live with it. You can call "apples" your mistakes, but the truth is, the "apple" is so much more than a mistake. Your life's apple has unseen consequences, because it grows up to be a tree with branches and roots, and it affects your whole life. That's the reason we call it a tree.

Think about it: There are mistakes people made when they were teenagers, which planted a seed in their life. Yes, they learned a lesson, so something good came out of it, but the outcome of it has become really far-reaching.

The impact of the occurrence is down at the core of who they are. The roots reach into the ground, and it essentially becomes a tree in their lives. It has become something they can't get rid of. Their action was a seed, but it went from being a seed to a tree.

If we take the time to think about our decisions before we make them, we should be asking ourselves the question, *"What are the long-term effects from making this decision? Am I solving a problem or creating another?"*

In conclusion, I ask you, what are the long-term effects of playing God to get what you want - a position, a child, a relationship? Think, think and think!

III

Don't Bite The Apple

The third part, **Don't Bite the Apple**, *addresses the consequences of "giving the forbidden apple a bite," which is to make a decision to follow our own path in life, instead of God's. Eve gave the apple a bite while Mary didn't. From the products of their conception, we learn that what we create or birth on earth, is a result of whether we bite the apple or not.*

8

WHAT SHOULD I EXPECT?

The creation waits in eager expectation for the sons of God to be revealed. **Romans 8:19-20, NIV**

In this chapter, I'd like us to examine the life of Eve, the wife of Adam in comparison to that of Mary, the mother of Jesus.

First, we see in Eve that double-mindedness that the devil introduces into her heart: *"Are you sure that the day you eat of this tree, you shall surely die?"* She begins to doubt what God had said to them.

Mary doesn't have such doubts. She does have a question, though. Her question, however, is not whether she's going to have a child or not. Mary does NOT disbelieve the fact that she will give birth to Christ. She doesn't act like Sarah at all. She does not laugh at the idea. She just ponders: "What kind of greeting is this?" In other words, "What should I expect?"

That was her response. And that should be our response when God tells us "Hey, I'm going to promote you to a certain position," or "I am going to help you start a business that'll make a great name."

Our question to God should be, "What should I expect?" It should not be disbelief. It should not be that a part of us believes that God will do it, and another thinks He won't. We shouldn't laugh or scorn at His Word because we think God waits too long to get anything done.

The simplest thing we should present before God is that we'd love to understand our role in the transaction: "Lord what should I expect in what you just told me?"

BAD DECISIONS

Next, we see that Eve is in the place of making the decision whether to eat the apple or not. She wants to make the decision to "be like God," which is what the enemy is deceiving her into.

Now notice something here: Adam and Eve were already created in the image of God. They were the image of 'Gods' on earth. The Psalmist said, "*I have said, **Ye are gods**; and all of you are children of the most High*" (Psalms 82:6). God had given Adam and Eve authority on earth. Psalms 115:16 says, "*The heaven, even the heavens, are the LORD'S: but the earth hath he given to the children of men.*"

In essence, Adam and Eve were angels on earth delivering the message of the Lord. Yet the devil said to them, "*For God doth know that in the day ye eat thereof, then your eyes shall be opened, and **ye shall be as gods**, knowing good and evil*" (Genesis 3:5). The devil was telling them that they can be in charge without God. He tried to separate them from their identity as the voice of God in the earth, in order to access and overwhelm their minds with his evil suggestion.

This is often the way the enemy operates. He first creates identity crises and then tries to dethrone God's Word from our hearts.

Let me use a situation many years ago in America to better illustrate this.

During the slave trade, the Americans went to get slaves from a country like India, but the entire country rose up against them. So, America couldn't take their people as slaves. But they were able to succeed in Africa. And the reason so many Africans were taken without a fight is because their African families had been dethroned. And you know, slavery is what happens next after you overcome or dethrone a people.

The Bible talks about how the children of Israel dethroned some inhabitants of a land and made them slaves. Joshua 16:10 says, *"The Canaanites living in Gezer were never driven out,* **so they still live as slaves among the people of Ephraim.***"*(TLB)

Some of the Africans were sold into slavery. Some were stolen and a yoke was placed around their neck. Some of them were royalty, asleep in their homes, and they were yanked out of their beds.

Now, the problem was, there was no place for the African Royal Families. Imagine Royalty like Prince William Ansah sessarakoo from Ghana, Princess Anta Madjiguene Ndiaye from Senegal, Prince Abdurahman Ibrahim Idn Sori from Guniea, just to name a few, being sold into slavery.

It's like deciding to dethrone everyone on the throne of England -

Countess, Princess, Baroness, Duchess, the Queen, the King, Parliament, and in fact, everyone in power – and sell them into slavery.

However, during the Jim Crow Era, one of the issues they had with the slaves was that they kept trying to run away. The issue was that these slaves knew who they were. So, they kept telling their children, "Hey, you are not a slave. You have your own land or you come from a lineage of kings and queens. You don't belong here." That became a huge problem for the slave owners.

To solve that problem, the slave owners began to separate parents from children, so the children wouldn't know who they really were. That separation from "who they are" would deprive or close them up regarding their identity and establish them in bondage.

That is the same method Satan uses. If he can separate you from understanding who you are, then he can both deceive and establish you perpetually in bondage. That is the same method he used on Eve. He tried to separate her from understanding who she really was, so he could easily deceive her into doing what God had prohibited them from doing.

At that point, Eve began to contemplate on the fruit. In making the decision to try the devil's suggestion, she began to see that the tree was good for food. Then she gave Adam the apple to bite. Genesis 3:6 says, *"And when the woman saw that the tree was good for food, and that it was pleasant to the eyes, and a tree to be desired to make one wise, she took of the fruit thereof, and did eat, and gave also unto her husband with her; and he did eat."*

GOOD DECISIONS

Mary was different. She didn't give her husband the apple to bite at all. She left that where it was supposed to be – completely up to God. So, God took it upon Himself to reveal to Joseph that what happened was of God.

Mary didn't even try to convince Joseph that it was the right thing to do. She let Joseph get a Word on his own, which is how it should be.

When you find yourself in Mary's kind of situation, you shouldn't be worrying over what is basically supposed to be God's business. Stay calm and let the other person get a Word from God over the situation.

If they're wondering, "Is this the right person I should be in covenant with?" they should get a Word from God over the situation. You shouldn't have to convince them like Eve and Sarah did to their husbands. You shouldn't have to do that. They should be able to, at some point, hear from God. Even if it's not initially, they should hear from Him eventually.

I'm sure Joseph had his doubts to handle at the initial stage. But after a certain point, he got exactly what God wanted for him.

You see, if that person you're considering is the one you're supposed to be connected to, God will give them a clear revelation, and you won't have to convince them.

Now watch what happens to Mary after she let God have His way!

CREATION AWAITS

In the process of time, Mary gave birth to God's promise in Ezekiel of one King, which is Christ Jesus. And you know what? The earth is waiting on us to do the same thing. Like Mary, we must give birth to the promise. Romans 8:19 says, *"The creation waits in eager expectation for the sons of God to be revealed."* NIV

Beloved, there is God's seed in you. His seed is His Word and plan for your life, and it manifests through the flesh. In other words, when God says you will give birth to a business, a book, etc., that is His seed. His Word over your life is His seed. Once you birth that business, that book, that Ministry, etc., they are counted as products of God's Word because the Spirit of God had descended upon it.

Don't forget that God dwells within you. But He can dwell within any matter; anything He created. That is why He can dwell within the pages of a book, and we say the book is anointed.

So, like Mary gave birth to God's seed within her, creation is waiting for you to give birth to God's seed within you. The earth is waiting to see you birth that great book, that wonderful business, that life-changing Ministry, that relationship, that marriage. The whole of creation is waiting!

I know the next logical question on your mind is, so when do I really give birth to my seed – my project, my idea, my marriage, etc.? When do I really proceed?

Well, let's see that in the next chapter.

9

DIVINE TIMING

Jesus saith unto her, Woman, what have I to do with thee? mine hour is not yet come. John 2:1 (NIV)

I need you to understand that there is a specific time for the accomplishment of every purpose. Solomon said in Ecclesiastes 3:1, *"There is a time for everything"* (NIV).

Even Jesus, while at the wedding in Cana, knew when it was His hour and when it was not. He understood Divine timing. You too must understand Divine timing. You must understand the difference between having a book, an idea or a concept and having it ordained by God. You must understand at what point your book, idea or concept is ready to be sent out to the masses.

Think about a man like David. He perfectly understood Divine timing. He knew his position. He knew that even though the previous king had a prophecy that ended his term abruptly, he couldn't dare pull up a sword and strike him. He knew too well that it was not his place to do that, but God's.

God moves people. You don't! Understanding what part you play and what part God plays is a big part of the puzzle. An apple tree can never become a pomegranate tree. A stolen blessing is not a blessing at all.

ANOINTED OR APPOINTED?

There is a bit of difference between being anointed and being appointed. Between the place of the anointing and that of the appointment is a process.

Jesus is revealed as having been the 'Seed of God' within the Father Himself. Luke 3:22 says, *"And the Holy Ghost descended in a bodily shape like a dove upon him, and a voice came from heaven, which said, Thou art my beloved Son; in thee I am well pleased."*

So, the Father says, "This is my Son 'or Seed' in whom I am well pleased," after the Holy Ghost descended upon Him in a bodily shape like a dove.

The question now is, wasn't He His (the Father's) Son before the Spirit descended upon Him? Of course, He was! He was the Seed of God, but the Holy Spirit had not rested upon Him. You see, you are supposed to be a tree of life, and true life has the Spirit of God within it.

Prior to this, our Lord was anointed but not appointed. He was chosen, and was Who God called Him to be, but He was not at the place of manifesting that call yet, until the Spirit came upon Him. No wonder the prophet Isaiah said, "**until at last the Spirit is poured out on us from heaven.** *Then the wilderness will become a fertile field, and the fertile field will yield bountiful crops*" (Isaiah 32:15, NLT)

The Spirit's descent on Jesus was basically like a multiplication of Him. It was like the story of Jesus Himself feeding the multitude, where He multiplied five loaves of bread and two fishes to satisfy 5,000 hungry men. The Spirit was designed to take Him to the masses. This is the moment that Christ enters into the fullness of Who He is supposed to be; Who God was grooming Him to be. At this point, He is the Tree of Life.

This is akin to what happened to David. He was anointed to be king of Israel, but he never assumed that office until it was due time. Yes, he was anointed, but he wasn't appointed unto that throne yet. Jesus also had been anointed, but he never had an appointment unto that position. But then His Kingship moment comes; that moment when God sends down the unction to make Him a Tree in the earth that has deep roots. God makes Him a Tree that everyone could eat of as described by Daniel. When you compare Genesis' description of the tree to that of Daniel, you see that Jesus is the restoration of that tree. He is the Tree of Life and he overcomes where Adam and Eve fail.

> Then **Jesus came with them to a place called The Garden of Gethsemane**, and said to His disciples, "Sit here while I go over there and pray." And He took with Him Peter and the two sons of Zebedee, and began to be grieved and distressed. Then He said to them, "My soul is deeply grieved, to the point of death; remain here and keep watch with Me." **Matthew 26:36-46** (NASB)

In other words, Jesus literally relived Genesis over again. That's why He said *"In the beginning was the Word..."* (John 1:1).

You would notice that immediately after His resurrection, He first went to the Garden to restore things. John 20:15 says, *""Woman," he said, "why are you crying? Who is it you are looking for?"* **Thinking he was the gardener,** *(Like Adam and Eve) she said, "Sir, if you have carried him away, tell me where you have put him, and I will get him."* NIV

The revelation of Jesus, therefore, brings restoration to the earth. So, you see that all God was trying to do was to restore our access to the Garden of Eden. All He wanted was to restore us to being who we were, previously. He wanted to restore our relationship with Him before we were born. He wanted to restore that intimate relationship that had been severed, broken and torn.

While all these were necessary and in the will of God, we see that Jesus walked in Divine timing. Even though He was anointed, He waited to be appointed to His position when the Holy Spirit descended on Him.

What that tells us is that there is a process in doing things. Sometimes we want to rush the process so we can get to our expected end, but there is always a revelation period. So, if you are willing to stop 'playing God,' and truly get God to be the Head of your life, your marketing team, your Ministry, your network, your business, then all else will fall in place.

GET CONNECTED

Have you ever thought about it? Why is it that many businesses never see the light of day? Why is it that many relationships never get to a good ending? Why is it that many books just end up on the shelf? Why do so many good ideas die in obscurity?

To perfectly understand how to get to the masses, you may need to have a good understanding of how God planned to reveal Christ to the world.

Here is the plan that the Bible lays out:

First, there is a Mary connection with John's mother, Elizabeth - a tribal or a kinship connection with someone who is also pregnant.

Second, John the Baptist reveals Christ and introduces Him to the masses.

These two observations point to the same thing:

You want to get connected to the masses? Look for people who are likeminded and get connected to them. Look for those who already bear God's anointing and testimony on their lives, not those who are trying to go about it on their own. Your connection must be with someone else who is also pregnant (anointed).

Like Mary, I am pregnant with Christ. I am pregnant with something that is anointed; something that will change the world. But I need to be able to connect with other people who are also pregnant with the will of God in their lives.

There must be a clear demarcation or separation from people who are busy playing God; people who are busy trying to manipulate their way into positions; people who are busy lying and cheating and stealing, all in the name of power.

We must be able to make the right connection, so that what we birth will become or grow into the Tree of Life in the earth.

10

SOUND OF THE TRUMPET

> *When the trumpets sounded, the people shouted, and at the sound of the trumpet, when the people gave a loud shout, the wall collapsed; so every man charged straight in, and they took the city.* **Joshua 6:20, NIV**

One of the things that Mary's life teaches us is how not to be double-minded in our lives or give birth to duality. Mary carried the seed of God just as we do. The Bible says, in 1 John 3:9 that *"No one who is born of God will continue to sin,* **because God's seed remains in him;"** NIV

The seeds of God are His Words, His plans, His thoughts, His voice. And the reality of it is, beloved, if we can recognize the seeds that are in our life, we can make change - real change - rather than just have the illusion or the shadow of change.

We must recognize the differences between the seeds of God and the seeds of Satan in our lives. That will ultimately decide if we become the Tree of Life in the earth or the tree of good and evil.

For some people, recognizing God's voice is simple and straightforward. For others, it's a long process. But we must accept that real revelation, sometimes, comes in stages. It can take forty days like that of Jesus in the wilderness or a person can wonder round and about the same issues like Moses for forty years. Sometimes, it all depends on the truth that we are willing to accept.

You know, a whole generation, because of their poor or wrong belief system, can be prevented from entering into the Promised Land on time. Deuteronomy 1:2 (NIV) says, *"(It takes eleven days to go from Horeb to Kadesh Barnea by the Mount Seir road.)"* So, a journey that should have taken eleven days for the children of Israel, which is a little beyond a week, stretched to forty years - almost half a lifetime.

You'd remember the story of the twelve spies recorded in the thirteenth chapter of the Book of Numbers. They were a group of Israelite leaders, one from each tribe, dispatched by Moses to scout out the land of Canaan for forty days. They were to bring back good report that aligned with what God had said. But ten of them went their own way, formed their own opinions, and returned with a bad report.

That bad report was a seed in their lives that grew into a tree that prevented them from getting into the Promised Land. They couldn't move forward because they were so busy believing their own lies instead of the Precious Word of God. Only two of the spies – Joshua and Caleb - stood on the side of God's Word, and their lives were different. Two of them made it into the Promised Land while the other ten perished in the wilderness.

Now I ask you: What seeds in your life are preventing you from receiving what God has promised you? Why aren't you moving forward in life? What lies have you believed that are preventing you from taking hold of God's promise?

I'm aware that there are common beliefs in all societies, groups, households, and even within religions. Many of such beliefs are seeds that grow up to be the tree of good and evil, when they should be helping you to be the Tree of Life that you're meant to be.
"You need to have 'connections' in order to be successful."

Ever heard that?

"It depends on who you know,..."

I know you've heard that.

"You have to have money to make money."

That's a very common one.

So, what are some beliefs that you put over the Word of God in your own life?

I counsel you to discard them from your heart. You can't put anything above God's Word and make any meaningful progress in life.

LISTEN TO GOD'S VOICE

Like the ten spies, what you believe affects the way you act. And what you believe stems from what you hear. Romans 10:17 says, "*The point is, Before you trust, **you have to listen**"* (MSG). So the question becomes, whose voice are you listening to? God's voice, your own voice or that of the snake in the Garden?

If you really intend to move forward with your life, you should try to recognize the voice of God. When you learn to recognize His voice, everything else will fall in place.

The Israelites at the base of the mountain likened God's voice to a trumpet. The trumpet is the seed, that is, the voice of God that makes things happen.

Here's a good example, a metaphor to help explain the trumpet so you can recognize it in your own life: There was a man named Michael Luther King Junior, who later changed his name to Martin Luther King Junior. He was a civil rights activist, but also a pastor. He had a simple message from the Father: "Let My People Go!"

Luther's message had the same theme like John the Baptist who seemingly gave the same message over and over again. No matter what wrapping paper he put around it, the core of the message was always the same: "Let My People Go!" His message introduced him to the world. People joined him in that cause, and they were all of one accord. They sounded a trumpet that bought down some of the laws that governed slavery.

CONCEPT OF DAY

You know, the slavery mindset isn't killed overnight. It's a process. That process is what the Bible calls *a day*.

You need to understand something about the 'day' in the plan of God. 2Peter 3:8(NIV) says, "*But do not forget this one thing, dear friends: With the Lord **a day** is like **a thousand years**, and **a thousand years** are like **a day**.*"

What does that mean?

It means that a day is simply a period of time that cannot be measured exactly within the timeframe of man. In other words, it is a season that man thinks a certain way, or a certain philosophy is accepted or believed to be true.

So, when you hear of *a day*, it could be a thousand years or one day.

You see the FIRST DAY that Martin Luther King Junior and his people had to deal with, was *the day*, or *the times* when slavery was born. People were sold into slavery and yokes were placed around their neck. Some were taken from their farms, others from their homes. Most royalties were dethroned and taken as slaves.

The second *day* were the days when slavery was accepted. It became a norm. People began to accept hideous ideas as just being normal. You know, there are things in our society that are wrong but we accept them because they are the norms of the time.

I'm sure you are getting to understand what *a day* is. It is the prevailing norm or a way of thinking.

In the third *day*, the North in America begins to impress upon the South that slavery is wrong. In other words, some people's eyes are opened to realize that these people are making profit out of slavery.

The fourth *day* is *today*. It is the day that slavery was abolished. But it was abolished without civil rights. So, what has become known as the Jim Crow Era meant that it was unlawful to have a slave. As a result, there was a hate because of losing money and the people who had once built their country.

You could compare this to the Biblical story of Moses, when his people were set free from slavery in Egypt. They moved out of Egypt with so much joy. The Red Sea parted and they walked on dry ground.

But not long after, the Egyptians began to chase after them, because they realized they had lost money and laborers. They knew they were now going to labor over what their slaves would have done.

That was the situation in America.

There was great hostility, especially in the South, towards the people they called '*Negros*' at the time. They felt they had lost something which was rightfully theirs, in the transaction. They now had to work instead of having someone else to work for them.

So, there was serious distaste and hate, because they felt they had the right to abuse these blacks, but the law was telling them that they didn't. They had to find other creative ways to abuse, lynch, and put fear into the blacks. In other words, they chased them like the Egyptians did the Israelites.

The next movement would be the Civil Rights Movement; and the Civil

Rights Movement is where Martin Luther King Junior comes into play. He comes in on the fifth day, having lived, at least, four other days through his family history.

He comes into the situation with a wide open, educated understanding that things needed to change, though not necessarily knowing how to change it.

Civil Rights Movement gave America some respect in the aspect of restoring equality. Even though it wasn't necessarily equal, it was simply better than what had existed. It did not give complete freedom, but it did give some basic human rights. It opened up some opportunities. It meant that you could pretend that racism wasn't a factor.

Now, did we still have some lynching? Of course! But we did make a head way.

The sixth *day* would be the day I will consider to be *right now*. And what we are in is what I call 'mock freedom.' *Mock freedom*, by my definition, is very similar to what we found in the Bible: It is a form of freedom, but it denies the power thereof.

2 Timothy 3:5 speaks about a form of godliness that denies the power thereof. Such 'godliness' often denies the real power of God in people's lives. It denies what God wants to do or what Christ came to do.

That really struck me, because I realized that freedom is also a form of godliness. And the thing with mock freedom is that it's not the way God wanted it.

If you look at it carefully, you'd see that the right not to digress is what we've now done. The right to education is what we have lost. The right to feel safe in the country is actually being threatened. The reality of it is, I've heard people say, "Go back home."

I was in a grocery store the other day, where I saw a Spanish young lady confronted by a white gentleman based on nothing, but her race. He told her that she needed to go back to her country. This young lady was hurt and shocked as anyone would have been, when you are minding your own business and someone feels like they have the right to interject their opinions in your life and spew venom. You could see that this man interjected his thoughts into her world just like a snake would.

He told her that she needed to go back home. And, of course, my mind went to the fact that he could go back home too. Without thinking, I moved in-between them and simply said, "You first go back to England, then we'll discuss her going back to a country that she may or may not even come from."

I said, "You're not even sure if she's Mexican." And of course, it turned out she was not Mexican.

You see, when people have hate, they see what they want to see. They think their misery is caused by someone else instead of realizing that they are the cause of their own misery.

It is my hope that of course, the next stage should be like the walls that come down in Jericho. That is the hope of day 7. How long it will take us to get there, I don't really know. But I'm sure you do get the idea.

All the explanations I have given so far are to help you understand that *a day* may not necessarily mean one day. And from all that is discussed, you can see that we are actually in the sixth day.

We don't seem to understand that sometimes what we think is the voice of God, is a way of thinking for us. You see, God is slowly walking us towards a better understanding of Himself, towards revelation. And it's not an "all at once" thing.

Unlike John the Revelator, who gets revelation of things in a short period of time, revelation for most people comes in days, in times, and in seasons. And when we all get in one accord, our voices become trumpets that sound what God is saying in that season.

For Martin Luther King Junior, when everyone came in one accord, they made a trumpet sound in America that said, "Let my people go!" In essence, trumpets are when God's people resound what God has already said. A trumpet is the voice of God through His vessels, which are you and me.

You see, there is nothing like having a group of people in one accord who make a loud sound. That's what was expected when Martin Luther King Junior and his people made a sound, the trumpet sounded and they spoke what God had declared.

It was like the case of Esau where Isaac said to him, "*You will live by the sword and you will serve your brother. But when you grow restless, you will throw his yoke from off your neck*" (Genesis 27:40, NIV). That is another way of saying, "When you get sick and tired of being a slave, you rise up and do something."

In its simplest form, there's a yoke around your neck; when you get tired of it, you're going to get rid of it. The reason why there's no change right now is because you're not tired of it. When you get tired of it, change will come. That's what Martin Luther King Junior represented. That's what Jesus represented.

Now, you will remember the story of Joshua and the Israelites marching round the high walls of Jericho to bring it down. God instructed them to have seven priests carry trumpets. The Bible says that Joshua and the children of Israel went round the city for six days, and on the seventh day, their trumpet brought down the walls.

You see, sometimes it takes a while before an issue is brought down. And this is the Bible's way of telling you that sometimes God doesn't solve a particular problem through one generation but several.

So then, Joshua bringing down the walls of Jericho in seven days represents the fact that certain situations might not be conquered all at once but gradually and ultimately.

So, don't give up just too soon on that situation in your life, because the walls will soon crumble, just like slavery crumbled in America. Just keep on with your prayers, your fasting, your intercession, etc. Soon, those walls will collapse at the sound of the trumpet.

WALK IN HIS PATH

Long before the walls of Jericho came crumbling down, something had happened.

Joshua 5:13-15(NIV) says, *"Now when Joshua was near Jericho, he looked up and saw a man standing in front of him with a drawn sword in his hand.*

Joshua went up to him and asked, "Are you for us or for our enemies?" "Neither," he replied, "but as commander of the army of the Lord I have now come." Then Joshua fell facedown to the ground in reverence, and asked him, "What message does my Lord have for his servant?" The commander of the Lord's army replied, "Take off your sandals, for the place where you are standing is holy." And Joshua did so."

What is happening here?

God tells Joshua to take off his sandals because the ground on which he stands is Holy. By implication, God is telling him, "Don't walk your path; walk the path that I have already pre-ordained."

Simply put, "You have to renounce your own path and follow My path."

Daniel told King Nebuchadnezzar something I'd like you to take note of, also. He said, "*You will be driven away from people and will live with the wild animals; you will eat grass like cattle. Seven times will pass by for you* **until you acknowledge that the Most High is sovereign over the kingdoms of men** *and gives them to anyone he wishes*" (Daniel 4:32, NIV).

So basically, all God needed was that Nebuchadnezzar would ACKNOWLEDGE that the Most High rules in the affairs of men. That's the good news. It's not something that is hard to do. You simply have to relinquish your authority. Yes, you are king, but you have to be king under God.

Like Joshua, you must take off your shoes and realize that you stand on holy ground where your path must be surrendered to His path; you stand on holy ground where your steps must be ordered.

You have to understand that even though you might find some success in doing things your way, that success would mostly come from manipulating your way into something. It'll end up as the tree of good and evil in the earth.

You need to trust God's choices for you instead of trying to force your way into relationships, friendships, companies, and businesses that God never meant for you to have. You need to follow God's path, and like David, wait to become king. Even when you have been anointed, you need to patiently wait until you are appointed, without trying to take advantage of any situation.

In conclusion, now that we know that we don't have to bite the apple, we can expect a trumpet in the earth that will sound and change the world.

Eve gave the apple a bite and gave birth to the tree of good and evil. Mary the mother of Jesus refused to bite the apple and gave birth to the Tree of Life.

In essence, what we create or birth is a result of whether we bite the apple or not. When we take the right decision like Mary did, we begin to give birth to the supernatural. But when we take Eve's decision and bite the apple, we begin to create things in the image of the flesh. It becomes a cycle where we make images of our own self.

That is why I say to you, Don't Bite That Apple!

But what happens if someone gave you the apple and unknowingly, like Adam, you bit it?

Then you need to re-evaluate your life.

So, I want you to look into your life and ask yourself, am I *a Mary* or *an Eve?*

Is this God or is this me?

Did God choose this relationship for me or did I play God and enter into a covenant with someone I should not have thought about?

Consider every decision you've ever made in your life. Was God in it or just you? Are you doing the job you're supposed to be doing or someone else's job? Did you start the company God wanted you to start or the company you wanted to start?

It's time to examine your life.

And then of course, the next thing is for you to begin to put those snakes out of your garden.

IV

Angels and Snakes

*The last part of the book, **Snakes and Angels**, is a profound exposition on how to put the "snakes" – the wrong voices and influences – out of our garden. It presents how to differentiate between the voice of the snake and that of God, which is the first major struggle of many people.*

11

SNAKES AND ANGELS

*She is a **tree of life** to those who embrace her; those who lay hold of her will be blessed.* **Proverbs 3:18** *(NIV)*

In the last chapter we saw several reasons why we should not 'bite that apple.' We saw reasons why we should choose the path of Mary the mother of Jesus, instead of that of Eve the wife of Adam, who took the snake's suggestion, bit the apple and also gave it to Adam.

In this chapter, our focus is on how to put the snakes out of our garden.

So, how do we put the snakes out of our garden?

I'd love to begin by looking at the temptation of Christ detailed in the Gospels. After being baptized by John the Baptist, Jesus goes on a fast for 40 days and 40 nights in the Judean desert. The objective is to get leadership direction; to know the will of God.

During this time, we read that Satan tempted Him, basically to abuse His power. That's a temptation that Judas, a few years later, would fall victim. Judas' temptation leads him to the downfall of his leadership.

Judas is misguided, misplaced and focused on his will. A look at how Judas ended shows that the Judases in our lives don't come back after they die. There is no death, burial and resurrection for Judas.

But Jesus, on the other hand, goes through death, burial, and resurrection.

Jesus has just been anointed with the Holy Spirit. He moves into the desert, a dry place, an uncertain place; a place without any expectation of water, to prove Himself. Jesus has just begun to walk into His purpose and has to find the will of God.

If you think for a moment Who Jesus Christ is, it brings to mind the question of how the same Jesus Who would later tell the Samaritan woman, that He had living water, finds Himself in a place of drought where He is uncertain; a place of conflict, where He cannot seem to produce the well within Himself.

This whole account is laid out in Matthew 4:1-11. However, I will focus on the words of Jesus and the interaction between Him and Satan. But I'll encourage that when you get a chance, you should read through verses 1-11 in its entirety, and it'll give you a better picture of what's going on.

Satan comes to Jesus and says, "If you are the Son of God, tell these stones to become bread."

Jesus replies, ""It is written: 'Man does not live on bread alone, but on every word that comes from the mouth of God.'"

Satan then says, ""If you are the Son of God, throw yourself down. For it is written: "'He will command his angels concerning you, and they will lift you up in their hands, so that you will not strike your foot against a stone.'"

Jesus turns again and says, ""It is also written: 'Do not put the Lord your God to the test.'"

Satan has one final word: "All this I will give you," he said, "if you will bow down and worship me."

Of course, Jesus' reply is, "Away from me, Satan! For it is written: 'Worship the Lord your God, and serve him only.'"

The above was Jesus' encounter with the devil. But as we see later on in His Ministry, Jesus at a point addressed Peter as Satan. Matthew 16:22-23 (NIV) says, "*Peter took him aside and began to rebuke him. "Never, Lord!" he said. "This shall never happen to you!" Jesus turned and said to Peter, **"Get behind me, Satan!** You are a stumbling block to me; you do not have in mind the things of God, but the things of men."* Peter was actually trying to save Jesus. He was trying to protect Jesus. But in doing so, Jesus called him 'satan.'

Jesus knew that Peter wasn't the one speaking at that point. He knew that the enemy was speaking through him. So, He was actually addressing the voice that spoke through Peter and not Peter as a person.

Note that just a moment earlier, Peter had given a revelation of Who Jesus was. Jesus stated clearly that Peter was speaking by the revelation of His Father in heaven. Matthew 16:15-18 (NIV) says, ""*But what about you?" he asked. "Who do you say I am?"* **Simon Peter answered, "You are the Christ, the Son of the living God.***" Jesus replied, "Blessed are you, Simon son of Jonah,* **for this was not revealed to you by man, but by my Father in heaven."**

Jesus tells Peter that His Father gave him the revelation of Who He is. A few moments later, He calls him Satan. From this, it becomes clear that we are exposed to two major influences or voices from which we have to choose.

MY STORY

When I was young, my mother asked a series of questions about the snake in the Garden. She said this couldn't have been the first time the same snake had spoken to Eve: "Wasn't Eve afraid of a talking snake?"

She wanted to know where Adam was, when the snake was doing all this talking to Eve.

The big question is, "Aren't snakes talking today?"

The truth is that the snakes are talking all the time. We just don't seem to recognize them as snakes. They are so ingrained in our culture that they talk to us all the time and we're neither surprised nor scared.

I will attempt to answer all the questions through sharing my childhood experience . That will become a reference point that we can use to point at the voice of the snake.

When I was about three years old, there was a hole in the wall, which was from the door knob that kept hitting the wall several times. There was no stopper on the door, so it made a hole in the wall. From time to time, there was a snake that talked non-stop. It always had something to say. I'm not sure if it was real or my imagination. But what I am sure of is that the snake's presence in my grandmother's room has been a lifetime memory for me.

But the snake wasn't alone; there was an angel in my room, too. She had a little Red Dog and he could fit in my hand. She would let me play with him most of the day. Often times, when my mother sent me to my room to play, she didn't realize it until later, that she was sending me to play with the angel and the snake, and of course, the Red Dog.

The angel would let me play with the little dog for hours. She would often disagree with what the snake had said. In other words, she always presented me a different perspective and, and most of the time it was the Angel's perspective that I listened to. The snake was in the wall at a distance but the Angel was in my room, right beside me.

You know, often times, as a child I would talk to the angel and then share with my mother what the angel and the snake had said. Most of the time, she would say I didn't focus on what the snake had said; that I only focused on what the angel had said.

The most vivid memory I have is the day the angel told me she had to leave, but that she would always be there; only that I wouldn't be able to see her. So, I ran to my mom with eyes full of tears, crying uncontrollably, because I felt like my best friend was leaving.

My mother would later let me know that she knew I had often been in the presence of an angel or an entity in there. She said she knew I wasn't making it up or playing make believe, because I spoke things that a three-year-old wouldn't have known to say.

When the angel was leaving, she made a comment to me that I would always remember. She said she would always be there even when I wouldn't see her, and even if I forgot her, she wouldn't forget me, and she would always be there to guide me and direct me throughout life.

From time to time in my life, I often thought about her.

Now, there was something more she said, which I wouldn't realize until my late 30's: that, even though she had said she would always be there, the snake would always be there, too. There were always two voices present in my life - the voice of the angel and the voice of the snake, but most of the time, the voice of the angel prevailed.

I lived that total experience in my grandmother's room with both the angel and the snake. Most of the time, I never really shared my childhood experience. I felt like Hermione Granger from the Harry Potter movie, when she tells Harry Potter - who had just heard the voice of a snake - that even in the world of magic, it's not okay to hear voices.

In the same vein, I know that even in the Christian world, where it is said that snakes were in the Garden talking, it is not acceptable to tell someone that you have actually seen a talking snake. I was told that my understanding of Genesis was a gift, but that I should keep it to myself. As I write this book, I have to overcome my will and write what I know, so I won't die and take the truth with me. I have children and I want them to be careful with their life and not *bite the Apple*.

I am guessing that other people may have a similar experience. I believe the only difference between what happened in my childhood and that of my growing up years is that, I was unable to see both the angel and the snake physically, but their voices would forever be with me. It was within me. It was in my friends and my family. It was in the culture. It was in every decision I made or didn't make. It was at every Cross Road. It was in the bad things that happened to me, and in the good things that happened in me.

Snakes and angels in my room was not just about me, even though I was too young to know the Biblical story of the Garden of Eden with the snake. I realized the Bible's narrative had some of the same characters in Genesis. The Bible doesn't call them angels, but rather, the voice of the Lord.

And, like the Bible's narrative of the snake and the voice of the Lord, I learn that there are many snakes and many angels around me. Sometimes the voices are in the things I read in commercials and in philosophies that are taught to me by others.

There were snakes and angels surrounding me and influencing my daily life. I was constantly listening to them. However, the challenge of putting the snakes out of my garden - which is my life - often seems like putting calories out of my diet.

THINK OF IT THIS WAY

Have you ever tried to lose weight? I mean, really try to lose weight. You look at all the labels. You try to eat only good fats. You put the app counter on your phone and the app for steps to keep track of your walking, to see how many calories you burn in a day. It doesn't seem easy learning new ways of eating.

You're in the kitchen trying to cook things that you have never eaten before. You're following vegan recipes. You're trying out foods that you may not really want to eat, all for the sake of changing your lifestyle. You want to live longer and healthier. You don't want to get to that point in your life where the doctors tell you that your health has badly declined, and you're going to die, all because you were so focused on making money and being successful, that you neglected your health.

I was watched the story, I believe it was called *Fat, Sick and Nearly Dead*. There was a gentleman from England, who was so financially successful. But his weight was so blown up that he was running into several health crises. The doctors told him that he would be in the grave by the end of the year. They told him to prepare to die. But he was so big that he would not even fit in a typical-sized casket if he died.

The idea of preparing for death was enough to scare him into a lifestyle change. What he did was, document his struggle in the lifestyle change, which was about him juicing his way to a healthier life. Basically, he juiced until he got to a certain weight, and once he got to that weight, he then began to eat salads and healthier foods. Then he lost almost 100 pounds.

One of the things he did to achieve his weight loss, was to take some time off, so that he doesn't get tempted, being surrounded by people who are steadily eating things that he shouldn't eat.

The journey that this gentleman takes, saves his life. He then comes to a place where he meets another gentleman, a truck driver, who has been given the same diagnosis, and he does not have the means or the money to change his lifestyle the way the British businessman did. The businessman does something I think is profound. He puts the truck driver up in a hotel and teaches him how to juice.

I believe he paid for the truck driver's hotel for 30 days. In 30 days, the truck driver lost between 50-80 pounds. At the end of 60 days, the truck driver had come down to a smaller weight. He received a second chance at life.

I share this story because I have done a similar juice fast and I understand the discipline it takes to change your lifestyle. It may be hard and difficult, but it can be done. You don't have to accept death. You can be disciplined about anything you set your mind to, from losing weight to not biting the apple.

Do you know what happens if you only do a little bit of dieting and then get back to eating your normal way? It's simple; you're going to put that weight right back on. To really lose weight and keep it off, you have to form new habits. You have to stop eating some of the things you really like – things like bread, processed foods, pies and cakes. You have to say 'NO' to McDonalds. And, when the light comes on at Krisby Kreme Donuts, you have to keep going.

I say that because I want you to feel the pain and difficulty of a lifestyle change. And, if you can feel that difficulty, then you can really begin to understand the journey it takes to putting these snakes out of your garden. The process is similar to putting calories out of your diet.

You will have to form new habits, watch the words you speak, and avoid the words of other people. You're going to be very disciplined, so that you can create a lifestyle change, and never return to the things you did

YOU ARE THAT TREE

before; because if you do, you will find your garden full of snakes again.

12

IDENTIFYING VOICES

When I was a child, I talked like a child, I thought like a child, I reasoned like a child. When I became a man, I put childish ways behind me. *1 Corinthians 13:11, NIV*

Now, the first thing people struggle with is how to know the difference between the voice of the snake and that of the angel. So, I want you to take that information about the snakes and angels, as well as the weight loss journey, and put it into a funnel, because I want to use our text to show how we may learn to identify the talking snakes or angels. That way, we can learn how to overcome the snakes in our garden and essentially put them out using God's Word.

I believe that we all want God's input on whatever He wants us to do. We want His input on what job we should take, where we should live, and even whom to marry. We want to know what His mind is on everything we want to do:

"Should I buy this house?"

"Should I move to Texas to start a business?"

We all have questions that we want God's input, and we all want to know His answers. But the reality is, God is never silent. If He is, it's because He's already given the answer.

To better identify the snake in our garden, let us examine the exchange between Satan and Jesus. But, instead of just thinking about the narrative between them, I want you to see and hear this as an internal exchange going on in the mind of Christ.

You can use the Bible to justify both sides of the argument.

Jesus actually gives us HIS first solution to identifying the voices, which of course, is to pray.

He also gives us a second solution, which is to fast for 40 days, so that we can hear the Words of God clearly. We can fast as a way to tell God that we want to separate our will from His will. In doing so, God gives us the strength as we spend intimate time with Him.

When we tell our flesh 'no to food,' we actually train the body to submit to the control of the spirit. Whenever the flesh expresses hunger, the spirit will rise up and say, 'NO, we are fasting.' By that we build an altar, which means that we send up our praise. We take off our shoes, meaning that we tell God, "Not my will, but Thine be done."

SOMETHING TO PONDER

Let me share an experience I had almost eleven years ago.

I was eight and a half months pregnant, roughly two weeks from the delivery when God gave me a premonition that my son had died. I woke up crying and praying, and I prayed for almost two hours. And you know, it was just me talking to God; it was not me listening. So, it was totally a one-way conversation.

After about two hours, I was able to calm myself down, while I asked God to save my son. So, I just stopped talking and sat there for a moment. I wanted to try to hear the words of God. He said one thing to me that I will never forget: He said, "If I give you what you want, are you willing to accept the consequences?"

I had never thought about the consequences of saving my child. I had asked for a good thing and God was talking to me about consequences. I was not pleased, to say the least. I had considered myself at that moment, to be a devout woman of God. I considered myself to be someone who tried to live up to His standards or at least, the standards the church had laid out for me.

For several years, I had been doing a reasonably good job at transforming my life, behaving myself, and doing good things. So, when I heard God speak, it felt like I was being punished. These were the thoughts that went through my head. They were the thoughts of a mother who had just been told by God that her child was going to die.

The reality of it is, if God was a man, you could argue a little more. But when God says a thing, you can't argue it out.

I was just furious - and that's my honest reaction. I was upset!

Some people will tell you that when God gave them such news, they were calm. Well, you know, I'm not sure what mindset they're in. I'm just telling you where I was. I was angry. I was upset. I was pissed. And all that anger was pointed at God, because it felt that I had done the right thing for the first time in a long time.

I had a span of seven or eight years that I was doing right in my mind. I was behaving myself. I had gotten rid of a lot of the things and habits I formed. I was being a good girl. But this time, I was fussing and ranting. I was verbal in ranting to God. I made comments in my anger; willful anger.

Of course, God didn't say anything.

Well, I finally said, "Nevertheless your will be done." And I went to bed angry and upset with God over His decision.

The next morning, I went to the doctor, and of course, they confirmed what God had told me. When they asked me why I was at the hospital emergency room, I told them the truth. I had all kinds of doctors. Everyone else would come to me and say, "I heard you had a premonition." I didn't necessarily have a word for it at that time.

There are experiences I've had that I may not necessarily have the terminology to explain. This was one of such. I just knew I talked with God. I would later hear people saying it over and over again, then I understood that what I had was a premonition.

People at the hospital were calling and visiting me. And they were coming to see me because I had a premonition. I was given a very negative lady doctor to check me. This was the same doctor I had seen previously during my pregnancy. I had told her I suspected that something was wrong, but she spoke as if I was completely ignorant. She said there was nothing wrong with the pregnancy and there was nothing wrong with the child. She believed my senses, if you will, were misguided. Well, she was the doctor, and of course, she knew better.

Now, when I showed up at her office, she pretended that we never had that conversation. When I first entered the office, she had an attitude, because I had gotten into the military emergency room to be checked. She was offended that I had come, with nothing more than a premonition from God, and no other signs of trauma.

I didn't have anything to report to her other than a premonition from God.

She was upset!

Nevertheless, when she discovered the truth, she delivered the news to me. But you know something? I was able to handle it without any form of provocation, because God had lessened the blow already by telling me about the situation before that time. So, when she told me, "Your son has no heartbeat," even though it still hurts, it was not as tough as it would have been, had God not told me.

To be honest, I had a real frank conversation with God when the doctor left the room. In my anger, I told Him, "If you're going to ask me to deal with, and endure this, you're going to have to give me someone to endure it with, better than this woman. I cannot deal with giving birth to a child that has died, with this woman. I will not go through this. You're going to have to make provision for me. I don't care where you move her, but she can't be here."

I spoke this loud, so that I was sure the nurses and the doctors could hear me as I was praying and having a real conversation with God. They probably thought I was a crazy woman. But, when someone delivers to you the news of the death of your child, it is enough to make a sane woman crazy. So, I didn't deny in that moment, the thought of people about me.

It just didn't matter, anyway.

Their opinion of my prayer, and of my relationship with God never mattered. This was about me and God; the rest of the world had disappeared into nothingness.

As I had a real conversation with God, it was maybe, an hour later that I was introduced to who would be my doctor, and he informed me that he would help deliver the child whom we later named, Timothy.

THE POINT

I'm sharing this story to help us understand that sometimes the VOICE we believe to be of the enemy is not necessarily the voice of Satan; it is sometimes the voice of God. The voice of God does not always bring you the GOOD news that you want. Sometimes the voice of God prepares you for what is coming ahead. It is like the person who gives weather forecast. He tells you what to expect.

The idea of my son's heart not beating was complicated in my spiritual life. To say I spent some years angry with God, would be an understatement. I suspect that I lost who I was in that moment; that day. There are pivotal moments in your life that when you come out on the other side, you're not the same person you were. I lost a lot of innocence that day.

You could perhaps, say that compared to most people, I am naive because I limit my exposure to certain things. It's not that I'm dumb, but rather that I choose to live a little differently. So, my perspective of things and my perspective of the world is perhaps, different. And the things I was exposed to, helped shape my perspective.

You have to come to the point in your life where you realize that, even when you pray, you don't pray to get your way anymore. That's one of the things that I grew up in faith to understand. Paul said in 1 Corinthians 13:11, *"When I was a child, I talked like a child, I thought like a child, I reasoned like a child. When I became a man, I put childish ways behind me"* (NIV).

I now understand there are consequences, so I don't pray to get my way anymore. Sometimes, I simply pray, "God's will be done," because I am reminded that there can be expected consequences.

13

IT'S ALL ABOUT HIS WILL

What is happening now has happened before, and what will happen in the future has happened before... **Ecclesiastes 3:15** *(NLT)*

Now, I want you to think back at something I described in an earlier chapter. That is the fact that God knew us before we were born. He knew us the way Adam new Eve; the way Abraham knew Sarah. And because He knew us, we conceived together "to make man in our own image" - the image of us and Him. We were in that creative process together.

That means we created every decision in our lives. And I need you to know that you are not trying to make a decision; you and God have already created the decision. You simply have to make the flesh carry out what you've already decided.

You remember in the Matrix movie – the second movie - when the oracle tells Neal, "You are not here to make a decision. You've already made the decision. You're just here to understand why you've made the decision."

That is the way it is with us.

You see, we're living in the now, but the future has already happened. The Bible says in Ecclesiastes 3:15 (NLT), **"What is happening now has happened before***, and what will happen in the future has happened before..."* It means we've already decided in the spirit realm. That decision has already been made in creation. We simply have to bring the decision into time.

If you choose to go against that decision, you have chosen to go against God's decision, that is, the agreement between you and God. The agreement was with God and was God's doing. There was nothing done outside of God. You and your spirit form connected with God in the spirit form and together you made or gave birth to man.

Man became pregnant with the mother of all living things that has the breath of life in them. In other words, we became pregnant in the way, the truth, and the light. Or better put, the answers of mankind.

So, we are pregnant with a solution for mankind.

YOUR WILL OR HIS WILL?

How do you know that God has made a decision about a matter?

Here's the truth about it: If you are in the midst of a decision and there is inward conflict, the conflict itself is a sign that you're stuck struggling between two choices. One choice is the tree of life, and the other is the tree of good and evil. There is no in-between.

Jesus makes it clear in what He says in the Garden (only that this time it's not the Garden of Eden, but the Garden of Gethsemane). He says to His Father, "Take this cup from me." Even though He knows that He has already agreed with God in the spirit to do this thing, His flesh wants to protect 'self.' His flesh wants to find a way to get out of the pain that He has to go through.

The Bible says in Luke 17:33 (NIV), "*Whoever tries to keep his life will lose it, and whoever loses his life will preserve it.*" Here we see Jesus trying to preserve His life. He has acknowledged that His spirit is willing but at this moment, His flesh is struggling to have its way. There seems to be a replay of the Garden of Eden here at the Garden of Gethsemane.

Jesus is trying to make that choice again. He's trying to struggle within Himself to become the Tree of Life rather than the tree of good and evil. He's trying not to preserve His life, but He is human right now. He is the Son of Man. But He must overcome His flesh to be the Son of God. In this moment, He is fighting the battle that every son of man must fight, to do the will of God over their own will.

After Jesus struggles in the Garden, He gives up just like I did when I was trying to save my son, Timothy. He just gives up His WILL and lays it down, like Eve and Adam and so many others before Him, should have done. He says, "*Nevertheless, thy will be done.*"

Now you can see clearly that the conflict is not about the choice, it is about you trying to get your way. The reason why you're conflicted is because you don't like His choice. That is where your struggle lies. When you're saying to God, "I don't know what you're really saying," what you really mean is, "God, don't you see the circumstances? How could you make this choice, looking at the circumstances?"

The point is that you think God should make a different choice for you, so you're arguing with Him. You're being like Jacob when he tells God, "I will not let you go until you, bless me."

But again, just like Jacob, if you get what you want, you're going to walk with a limp the rest of your life. Jacob got what he wanted, but there was a consequence. It's Just like God said to me, "Are you willing to accept the consequences, if I give you what you want?"

In essence then, what you are trying to do is to have your WILL implemented. You're trying to get things your way. So when you say, "I don't know what choice to make," you are not telling the truth. You know it, but you are just struggling with it. The thing is that, you must kill your will, and sometimes that means you must not try to save your life, or protect yourself. You must get rid of all the 'what if's'

Your fears are now misplaced when you don't do something because you're worried that you may get hurt in the process. IT'S NOT ABOUT YOU; IT'S ABOUT THE WILL AND PLAN OF GOD.

WHAT IS YOUR FOCUS?

The question that faces us now is, what's our focus? Are we focusing on protecting ourselves rather than focusing on the work that needs to be done?

Listen, Satan wants you to focus on saving yourself, promoting yourself, and making yourself important. On the other hand, the course of God is about sacrifice, the bigger picture, the work that needs to be done in the kingdom. God wants you to help other people and see the good that can come from it.

Let me give you an example. You're in a marriage, or a relationship, and God wants you to stay in the relationship but you're saying to Him, "God, don't you know the pain that this relationship is causing me?" You feel that God should feel the way you feel 'used.' You say you want to protect mummy's baby. I perfectly understand. But is that more important than being a light in someone's life. You have to see the big picture.

I make the same mistakes: I get hurt, and I'm fearful just like you are. I want to protect mummy's baby just like you do. But the reality of it is, what you're struggling with is not the decision of whether you should keep the relationship or not. You know, you aren't going to be hurt in the process, if you focus on becoming a light to the people in your life and giving them love. If you focus on that, it's easy to see that you're trying to get YOUR will to play out. That is what you are really struggling with.

But you must focus on the bigger picture!

The question is, "What are you conflicted about right now?"

In that conflict is an answer that God has already provided. You and God have already come in agreement in the spirit.

What you are trying to figure out is, "Can I save my flesh, and get what I want?"

Your conflict is God's way of letting you know that you and Him have already made a decision about that thing in your life. So, for instance, you know the right person you're supposed to be with. You know the right job for you. You already know if you should make that move.

The conflict is you trying to figure out why you made that decision, with the feeling of death so closely related to it. That's because your flesh thinks that decision puts you at risk.

In order for you to make the right decision, you're going to have to learn to overcome the voice of the snakes that are talking to you in your garden. It doesn't matter if the snake is within you or within your co-worker. 2 Corinthians 10:5 (NIV) says, "*We demolish arguments and every pretension that sets itself up against the knowledge of God, **and we take captive every thought to make it obedient to Christ.**"*

In conclusion, we all live with the voices of angels and the voices of snakes on a day-to-day basis. Perhaps like me, at a young age, you lost your ability to clearly recognize the angels of God, you can train yourself to see them in your garden, from the conflict within you about the decisions that you've already made, to the conflict that you will undoubtedly experience.

You can overcome your fears, your innate ability to want to save yourself and instead, sacrifice your life and your will for His plan.

It's true, you might get heartbroken. It's true you may have to hang on a tree like Jesus, because you disrupted the plans of the Enemy. They might come to crucify you because of your impact. But you don't have to become the serpent in the story. You don't have to become the serpent in someone else's life. You can be the voice of the angel in your life, you can be the voice of the angel in others' life, and you can generally be the voice of God in the earth.

All you have to do is pay attention to the labels on the products you consume for knowledge and wisdom. Pay attention to the options in your life, so you could exercise your faith, and you can win if you don't give up.

Proverbs 3:13-18 (NIV) says, "*Blessed is the man who finds wisdom, the man who gains understanding, for she is more profitable than silver and yields better returns than gold. She is more precious than rubies; nothing you desire can compare with her. Long life is in her right hand; in her left hand are riches and honor. Her ways are pleasant ways, and all her paths are peace.* **She is a tree of life** *to those who embrace her; those who lay hold of her will be blessed.*

Remember that God has already created a plan where you have a death, burial, and resurrection, and that plan will change the world. You and God have created man to walk out the image and the picture of God. That picture is the tree of life.

And you are that tree!